Count Our
COUNTRY'S
CHANGE

By Barbara Kramer

CELEBRATION PRESS
Pearson Learning Group

Contents

Coins Are Everywhere

Plink, plink. A girl drops coins into a piggy bank. She is saving to buy something special.

At a store, another girl pays for her purchases with a ten-dollar bill. Her change is one dollar and twenty-four cents. The cashier hands the girl a dollar bill, two dimes, and four pennies.

A boy buys juice from a machine. The cost is seventy-five cents. He drops three quarters into the slot—twenty-five, fifty, seventy-five cents.

People handle coins in many situations.

A Piggy Bank?

People often save coins in small banks shaped like a pig. Why a pig? In the fifteenth century, a special type of clay called *pygg* was used to make jars and pots. People who wanted to save a little money tossed coins into one of those jars. They became known as pygg jars. Later, clay banks were made in the shape of a pig, probably because the words *pygg* and *pig* were so much alike.

We use a variety of coins in our daily lives. They include pennies, nickels, dimes, quarters, half-dollars, and even dollars. Where do we get all those coins? They are made at special factories called mints.

The word *mint* comes from *mynet*, the Old English word for money. That was later shortened to *mynt*. There are mints all around the world, where each country makes its own coins.

The British Royal Mint has been housed in several places, from the Tower of London to the building shown here to a newer building in Wales.

Base 10

Countries have different **monetary** systems. The U.S. uses a base 10 system. For example, a dollar is equal to 10 dimes or 100 pennies. Because it is a base 10 system, money can be written as decimals to show different **denominations**.

Coin	Decimal
penny	$ .01
nickel	$ .05
dime	$ .10
quarter	$ .25
half-dollar	$ .50
dollar	$1.00

Great Britain once used a base 12 monetary system. There were 12 pence to a shilling and 240 pence to a pound. In 1971, Great Britain switched to base 10. Now, 100 pence equals 1 pound.

The U.S. Mint

In the United States, the first National Mint was built in 1792 in Philadelphia. At that time, Philadelphia was the nation's capital. Now, there are four U.S. Mints where coins are made. They are located in Philadelphia, San Francisco, Denver, and West Point. The Mints are part of the U.S. Department of the Treasury. They make only coins. Paper money is made by the Bureau of Engraving and Printing in Washington, D.C.

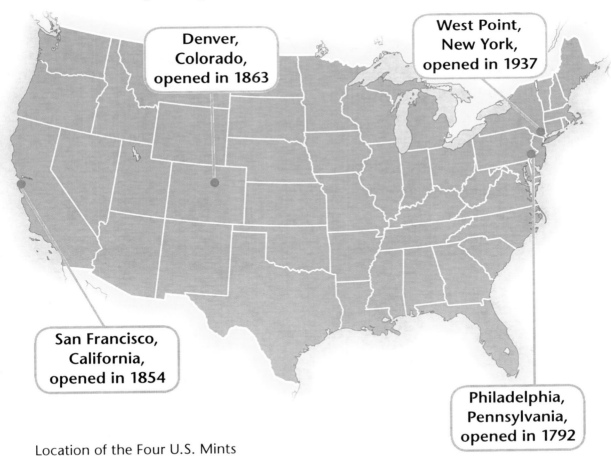

Denver, Colorado, opened in 1863

West Point, New York, opened in 1937

San Francisco, California, opened in 1854

Philadelphia, Pennsylvania, opened in 1792

Location of the Four U.S. Mints

Different Types of Coins

The coins we use every day are called circulating coins. They circulate, or travel, from one person to another. All of those coins are made at the Philadelphia and Denver Mints.

Mints also make **commemorative** coins to honor a person, place, or event. The first of these coins was manufactured in 1892 in honor of Christopher Columbus. Other coins were made to celebrate the Olympic Games and the 100th anniversary of the Statue of Liberty.

Circulating coins include a penny, a nickel, a dime, a quarter, a half-dollar, and a one-dollar coin.

This 1976 quarter was created in honor of the 200th anniversary of America's independence.

a set of commemorative coins showing endangered species

State Quarters

Some commemorative coins also circulate. An example is the state quarters program. In 1999, the U.S. Mint began producing quarters that have a special design on the back to honor each state. Each state helped create the design for its own quarter.

New state quarters were introduced every ten weeks with the last quarters minted in 2008. The coins were released in the order in which the states joined the Union. The Mint produces about 450 million of each state quarter.

Louisiana state quarters

Congressional Medal of Honor

Purple Heart

Other Work at the Mints

The Mints manufacture special sets of coins for people who collect them. They also make national medals. One is the Congressional Gold Medal. It is used to honor great Americans. Other medals include the Bronze Star, the Purple Heart, and the Congressional Medal of Honor. They are awarded to military heroes.

The Philadelphia Mint is the largest mint in the world.

front and back of commemorative silver dollars celebrating Benjamin Franklin's 300th birthday

Making Coins

The Philadelphia Mint is the largest mint in the world. It makes more than 30 million coins a day. It is a noisy place with large machines all banging and clanging at once.

Blanking

The first step in making most coins is called blanking. The Mint buys strips of metal about 13 inches wide and about 500 yards long. That is the length of five football fields lined up end to end. The metal is about as thick as the finished coin will be. Dimes are the thinnest coins.

One coil of metal is large enough to make 325,000 nickels.

The strips come to the Mint rolled into large coils. One coil weighs about 6,000 pounds, or 3 tons.

The coil is loaded onto a wheel. Then, the metal is fed into a machine called a blanking press. That powerful machine acts like a giant cookie cutter for coins. It slams down on the metal, punching out blanks that tumble into bins.

Webbing

The metal left over after the blanks are punched out is called webbing. It is shredded and recycled to make new sheets of metal.

Heat, Wash, and Dry

Next, the blanks are heated in a furnace to make them soft. Then, they are dropped into a tank to cool.

Heating turns the blanks a grayish color. So, the next step is to run them through a washing machine. The blanks are soaked and spun in a mixture of chemicals. Then, they go to the dryer.

A large tube called a whirlaway takes the blanks to the washing and drying station.

The washing machine makes the blanks bright and shiny again.

Riddling

The next stop is the riddling machine. Here, the blanks are shaken on a screen. It weeds out any blanks that are the wrong size or shape.

Upsetting

Then, the blanks move on to the next stage, called upsetting. The upsetting mill puts a raised rim all around the edge of the blank on both sides. That helps protect the design from wear. It also makes the coin last longer. The blanks, at this stage, are called planchets.

A raised edge on coins helps to protect the design from wear.

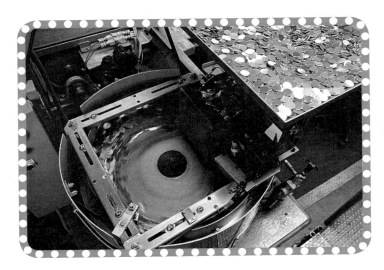

the upsetting mill

Reeding

At this time, reeding—or grooves—are added to the outside edge of some coins. Dollars, half-dollars, quarters, and dimes were once made from gold and silver. Because those metals were so valuable, some people shaved off the edges of the coins. They melted down the metal to sell. Reeding was added to prevent people from damaging the coins.

Reeding

How Many Reeds?

The number of reeds on a coin varies.

Coin	Number of Reeds
dime	118
quarter	119
half-dollar	150

Pennies and nickels were made from copper and nickel. Since those metals were not as valuable, those coins have smooth edges. Today, coins are an **alloy**, or mixture, of less valuable metals. However, the reeding is still useful. It helps visually impaired people identify the coins by touch.

Is a Nickel Made of Nickel?

It one time, all U.S. coins were required by law to be made of gold, silver, or copper. That became too expensive as the price of gold and silver rose. Now, all coins are made of a combination of metals.

pennies: zinc with a copper coating
nickels: a combination of copper and nickel
dimes, quarters, half-dollars: a core, or inner part, of copper; a coating, or outside layer, of copper and nickel

A Golden Dollar?

In 2000, a new golden dollar was introduced. The coin has a portrait of Sacagawea on the front. She was the young Shoshone woman who helped Lewis and Clark explore the Louisiana Territory. The golden dollar is not really gold at all. Instead, it is made of a special alloy of metals that makes it appear gold.

Striking

The next step in the coin-making process is to imprint the planchets with a design. This is called striking.

The planchets are fed into a stamping press. Both sides are stamped at once between sets of **dies**. One die stays in place while the other one strikes the other side. The planchet is now a coin. Usually the die that stays in place is the back or "tails" side of the coin. The one that strikes against the coin is the "heads" side.

dies ready to imprint the side of a planchet

How Many Coins Does One Press Strike?

A stamping press can strike about 750 coins per minute. If it was printing dimes, how much money would it strike in a minute? If it was striking pennies, how much money would that be in a minute? How many coins can it strike in an hour? (answers on page 23)

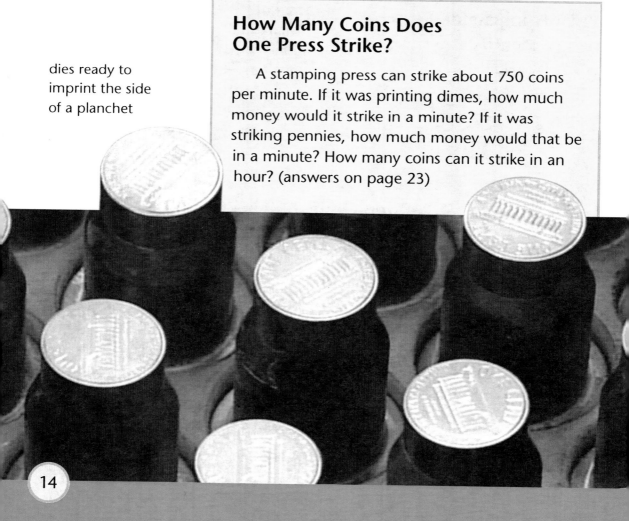

14

Putting a Face on It

Designs printed on the front of circulating coins have changed over the years. Early pennies showed the head of an imaginary woman with long flowing hair. She was known as Lady Liberty. She also appeared on other coins.

Today, circulating coins all show the head of a famous person on the front. Most of them are presidents.

When did these presidential faces first appear on current circulating coins?

Lady Liberty on the front of an old coin called a "half dime"

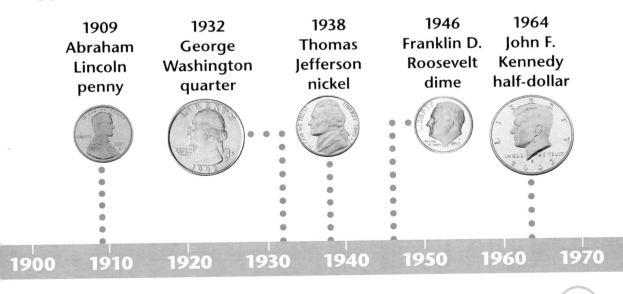

1909 Abraham Lincoln penny	1932 George Washington quarter	1938 Thomas Jefferson nickel	1946 Franklin D. Roosevelt dime	1964 John F. Kennedy half-dollar

1900   1910   1920   1930   1940   1950   1960   1970

Creating a Design

Designing a new coin starts with an artist who makes a drawing. Then, an engraver makes a clay model of the coin. It is much larger than the coin will be.

The model goes to the transfer-engraving machine. It reduces the design to the size of the actual coin. It also uses a sharp tool to carve the design into a steel **hub**. It takes more than 24 hours to carve one side with total precision. It takes just as long to do the other side. Then, the hubs are used to make pairs of metal dies for stamping the coins.

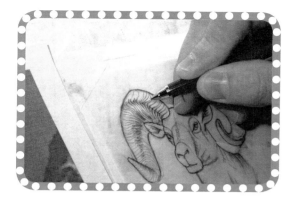

An artist sketches a new coin design.

A large model of the coin is made.

An engraver works on the engraving design.

Features on All Coins

U.S. coins have different designs, but they are also alike in some ways. Two **mottos** must be printed on all circulating coins. They are *In God We Trust* and the Latin phrase *E Pluribus Unum,* which means "out of many, one." It refers to the fact that the United States was formed by people from many states who united as one. The words *Liberty* and *United States of America* must also appear on each coin.

Many coins have a small letter such as a *D* or a *P*. The letter represents the U.S. Mint where the coin was made.

Liberty

motto

year

mint initial

country

motto

coin denomination

Only the Best

After the coins are printed, they fall into a bin called a trap. An inspector uses a magnifying glass to examine the coins. There is not enough time to handle every coin. So, it is a **random** check.

Coins that do not meet the standards of the U.S. Mint are sent to a machine called a waffler. This piece of equipment has large rollers that make ridges across the design on the coins. The ridges make the coins no longer usable. Later, the metal from those coins is recycled to make new metal strips.

A magnifying glass can reveal coins that don't meet the U.S. Mint's standards.

An inspector examines the coins.

If the coins meet all the standards, the inspector pulls a lever. The coins drop out of the bin and onto a conveyor belt. It takes the coins to a machine that counts and bags them. A scale weighs the canvas bags to make sure each one contains the right amount of coins. The bags are sealed and stored in a **vault** until they are needed by a Federal **Reserve** Bank.

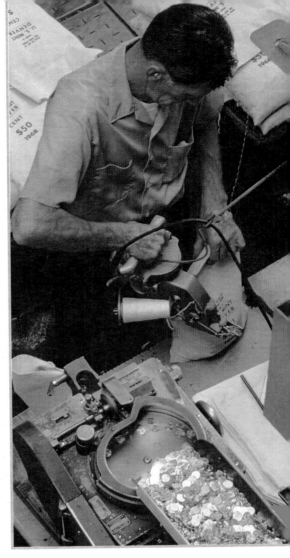

Coins are counted by an automatic counting machine.

A worker at the Denver Mint seals a bag of pennies.

Money Bags

A bag of pennies from the U.S. Mint is worth $50.00. How many pennies does it take to fill the bag? A bag of dimes is equal to $1,000. How many dimes are in the bag? (answers on page 23)

Coming to a Bank Near You

There are twelve Federal Reserve Banks located across the United States. They distribute money to private banks in their regions.

Pennies and nickels are shipped in tractor trailers from the Mints to Federal Reserve Banks. Other coins are usually shipped in armored trucks.

When a bank in your town needs coins, it can buy them from the Federal Reserve Bank. Each bank has a checking account with the Federal Reserve Bank in their area. Sometimes, banks end up with too many coins. In that case, they send extra coins back to the Federal Reserve Bank. Their accounts are credited for the amount of coins they return.

San Francisco

Federal Reserve Bank, San Francisco, California

Location of the Twelve Federal Reserve Banks in the United States

Federal Reserve Bank, Chicago, Illinois

Federal Reserve Bank, New York, New York

Minneapolis

Boston

Chicago

Cleveland

New York City

Philadelphia

Kansas City

St. Louis

Richmond

Atlanta

Dallas

Federal Reserve Bank, Minneapolis, Minnesota

The Federal Reserve Bank stores the coins in its vaults until they are needed again. It also sorts through the coins to weed out those that are bent or too worn to be used. The average lifespan of a coin is 30 years. Old coins are shipped back to the Mint. They are melted down to make new metal strips. Then, the coin-making cycle begins again.

It costs the U.S. Mint more than a cent to produce each penny. Still, most Americans want to keep pennies in circulation, like other coins.

Glossary

alloy   a mixture of two or more metals

commemorative   preserving or honoring the memory of a person, place, or event

denominations   classes or kinds of monetary units

dies   metal pieces with designs engraved on them used for stamping coins

hub   a steel blank with the design of one side of a coin carved into it

monetary   having to do with money

mottos   sayings or expressions that show the beliefs of a person or group of people

random   done without a clear pattern; selected by chance

reserve   the actual cash in a bank or assets that can be turned into cash quickly; to keep back or hold over

vault   a room designed to keep valuable items safe

Answers to Problems
p. 14: $75.00; $7.50; 45,000 coins
p. 19: 5,000 pennies; 10,000 dimes

Index